I0170048

Limericks, Odes and Poems (LOP)

Gillian Kay

illustrations by Mary Patrick

III Clink Street

London | New York

Published by Clink Street Publishing 2020

Copyright © 2020

First edition.

The author asserts the moral right under the Copyright, Designs and Patents Act 1988 to be identified as the author of this work.

All rights reserved. No part of this publication may be reproduced, stored in a retrieval system or transmitted, in any form or by any means without the prior consent of the author, nor be otherwise circulated in any form of binding or cover other than that with which it is published and without a similar condition being imposed on the subsequent purchaser.

ISBN:
978-1-913962-30-2 - paperback
978-1-913962-31-9 - ebook

Foreword

This little book is a bit of a journey over a number of years. These are observations on life, small as well as the larger political moments, including the desperate route through Lockdown. Some may make you smile, even laugh, others might bring a tear. We hope you enjoy our reflections on the ups and downs of life.

Contents

LOP ON
WOMEN

Dora

Dora was grizzled
I thought she was frizzled
She had never taken a man to bed
At least that's what they said
Until she met Dan, the desperate man
And Dora was changed from grizzled to glam

Twig of a woman

She was a twig of a woman
With very big hair
Nails like daggers
And shoes on ladders
I thought she was quite smart
'til she did a big fart!

OOPS...!

Ageing

I woke up one day
To find my left breast had gone away
My right one was holding on
But I knew it would soon be gone

They say that as you get older
You get a lot less bolder
Instead you find some inner peace
So I searched on the beach and craggy heath

I went to the mall
With no luck at all
I went to the church
But it was closed for brunch

So I tried Buddha, Allah and zen
But found them all to be men
I even asked a man called Fred
Gave up and went to bed

LOP ON
FAMILY

The dodgy knee

My mother has a dodgy knee
She is generally as fit as a flea
The knee can move quite quickly
Although at times it can be tricky
If you don't phone or call
The knee will not move at all

I visited my mum

It was fun to see the dodgy knee
Paddling about in the foam of the sea
It had been quite a bad spell
So it was good to see it looking well
The knee is quite bright and trendy
And sometimes can be very bendy
I stayed with the knee a week or so
It gave me such a wonderful glow

LOP ON
ANIMALS

The tiger is extinct

The tiger is extinct
It created quite a stink
The boy tiger was as mad as hell
'cause he couldn't find a gel

Some monkeys are quite rare
But I don't think many people care
Elephants are fun
But they are also nearly done

The tiger looked from side to side
But couldn't find a bride
He gave up his fruitless quest
And married a big striped vest

Maggie and Oscar

Maggie is a lovely dog
Walks through bogs and even fog
Oscar is a grumpy cat
Eats too much and is very fat
Maggie loves to play
Oscar just sits all day
Maggie likes lots of love
Oscar would rather kill a dove

Susan

I was as mad as hell when Susan died
The culprit marten, should have been tried
He didn't seem to care a jot
Susan lay dying on the spot

Protected pine martens might be
Susan never saw him in the tree
Never mind the pine marten's plight
What about Susan's RIGHT TO LIFE!

Susan was a beautiful hen
Not bothering anyone in her pen
It's such a shame she died that way
While marten lives to kill another day.

The mice are eating my car

The mice are eating my car
I'm not joking they really are
So far they have eaten padding
And lots of bits are now sagging

They have eaten through the turbocharger
There really is no harbour
They have moved on to the fuel pipe
I really have one big gripe

I am definitely and properly stuck
My car is still a sitting duck
I'm going to sit up every night
Preparing for a mouse gunfight

There's more to a midge

The Scottish midge is least understood
It's not just a bug looking for food
There's more to the midge than most folk know
They don't just bite no, no, no

Their ideal houses are built in groups
Cause they live in large family troops
Donald was the oldest son
His brothers numbered a thousand and one

Mary was the youngest and quite confused
The people she bit were left bemused
Colin was camp and gay
The midges thought he was cool that way

So next time you get a bite from a Scottish midge
Don't just squash it and make it go squidge
Have a heart and don't be a cad
Everything has a mum and a dad

COLIN

Donald's story

Donald hung about the pubs a lot
To bite the drunks on any spot
He would bite on face and neck and trunk
Until he also got very drunk

The other midges were all a buzz
They thought he was a drunken fuzz
Indeed, he was but he didn't care
He thought they were all unfair

He carried on without a thought
Saying to himself f… the lot
Then one night he got too frisky
And drowned in a glass of Glenmorangie…

COLIN AGAIN   DONALD

The Interview

The squirrel and I had a one to one
It was serious interviewing and not for fun
What are your ambitions, I asked politely?
To eat lots of nuts and go lightly

Also I will get access to a posher garden
I'm sorry, I beg your pardon?
I can get a better class of nut
It will be much better for my gut

What's been your greatest fear?
Being eaten by a pine marten that's got too near
What's been your greatest achievement?
Not being eaten and no bereavement

What will you do on your first day?
Eat as many nuts as in the month of May
Nuts can't be your only ambition?
Why not it's a serious mission?

Do you think you should get the job?
Yes, definitely I'm different from the mob
OK I will take a chance and give you work
Don't let me down and do not shirk

The squirrel worked hard every day
He skipped and hopped in every way
He got high-class nuts and much, much, more.
The Red Squirrel Café never shut its door.

LOP ON
HEALTH

Your own mind

It's important to know your own mind
Otherwise it's a bit of a bind
I met mine yesterday and then it went away
I definitely lost mine for a while
Then I found some bits by a style
I found some more by a bend
And feel much more on the mend

Depressed mouse

There is a depressed mouse in our house
It's definitely a mouse and not a louse
It's in the drawer where we keep the pills
We think it's suffering from some ills
It seems to favour vitamins c and d
Although occasionally it will go for e
It comes and goes in the dead of night
And gives us both quite a fright

LOP ON RELATIONSHIPS

Clive

I met a man called Clive
It was hard to tell if he was alive
He didn't drink or smoke
And was an all-round good bloke

He always ate at seven
And never went to bed after eleven
He knew a lot as well
And was just such a swell

He had much to say
And worked hard every day
I thought I was in real luck
'til I realised he was a boring f...

Pete

Then I met a man called Pete
He really was quite neat
He drank and smoked
Oh what a bloke
He certainly knew he was alive
And not a bit like Clive
Then he went a bit funny
And ran off with all my money

Stan

When I met Stan
I thought he was the man
Then he got a tan
And ran off with Fran

Clive again

I tried Clive again
Probably the best of those men
He had his own money
And didn't do anything funny

At first it was quite good
He was always in the same mood
Always there for me
And always making tea

Then I said let's eat at nine
He turned a strange colour of lime
Once he recovered from that
For the last time I left his flat

LOP ON
INSTITUTIONS

The Pension

I never thought a pension
Could cause so much tension
Lots of calls and letters written
We really got quite hard and bitten
Then my husband lost the plot
Got a gun and shot the lot

Eggs and baskets

My father used to say
Until his dying day
Never put your eggs in just one basket
Not even in a very large casket

So I got lots of baskets and lots of eggs
Some of them even grew legs
Then I got dementia of the mind
And a single egg I couldn't find!

The insurance company

The insurance company said it was good to pay
Just in case I got ill some day
They said it would give me peace of mind
And the insurance man was very kind

Then one day I got quite ill
The doctor gave me a big blue pill
I didn't seem to get any better
So I wrote the insurance company a letter

The insurance company said they wouldn't pay
But they would send a man out the next day
Instead of being kind, the man was quite nasty
I hope he ends up as mince in a pasty

The Helpline

My phone is working but my broadband is not
To begin with I was ok and not distraught
I phoned to report the fault on the helpline
All operators were busy so I had a glass of wine

I put my phone on to speaker mode
To go about my business and not be slowed
Message said report the fault on their website
I thought I don't have internet for that insight

I persisted and kept holding on
Then a voice 'Can I help, my name is John'
My broadband is not working I replied
On the website you will find a guide

My internet is not working, that's absurd
Ok I need your user ID, PIN and password
I don't have these details my network is down
I can't get your file and sorry if you frown

Ok I will move to another provider
Your contract doesn't end you can't be a rough rider
I thought you couldn't see my file
No need to be so hostile

Is this a helpline I asked politely
Not at all he said brightly
I thought I don't have this time
Hung up and had more wine.

My parcel is missing

My parcel is lost
Oh what a cost
My tracking number is long
Still that means it's strong

Seventeen numbers, I put them all in
It made my head truly spin
I had to open an account
To find my parcel and get the discount

The account reference had 15 digits
I thought this is getting vicious
Still I saw my parcel was not on track
It would never be coming back

So I decided to complain
I put all the numbers in
But forgot the password and the PIN
Reset them so I could begin
Finally, my complaint was duly noted
I got another reference that I never quoted
I really, really don't care anymore
All these numbers are such a bore

LOP ON
POLITICS

There's a very big hole

There's a very big hole in the ozone
That stops the ice being frozen
There's a very big hole in the ground
Where a thousand bodies were found
Still if I leave it 'til tomorrow
I won't need to bother

My God will judge
(My God is better than your God)

There were no weapons and we all knew
But your lies just grew and grew
We went to the streets and told you so
Then we found out and that was a blow

Then you said sorry and that was ok
You didn't mean guns, you meant **regime anyway**
That's illegal so we didn't like that
And you guys said sorry and oh dear drat

Then you said your God will judge
We think that's one big fudge
All the worlds have their Gods too
And they might take a different view

Very annoying indeed

It is very annoying indeed
When people don't realise they are freed
We went to a whole lot of trouble
And people have made it one big muddle

It is very annoying indeed
When some folks talk about greed
We did the demolition after all
It's only fair that we build back the wall

It is very annoying indeed
When people challenge the obvious lead
The leaders greet and meet
While ordinary folk took to the street

It is very annoying indeed
When the leaders are so steeped
When we didn't sit on the fence
We knew the intelligence made no sense

Shame the leaders have just found out now
I don't think they deserve a bow
Maybe we should pity them for being so slow
Maybe not, lets hope they go
It's very annoying indeed.

Leaders are supposed to be...

Leaders are supposed to be kind and brave
Their responsibilities are very grave
They're thoughtful and considered
Always calm, never embittered

Their wisdom is strong and true
They will never ever forsake you
Lies and greed are not their trade
History never lets them fade

Never take us to war on unchecked notes
And let young men die in tanks and boats
They would never be part of bribes and greed
Not even for Lords would they concede

I've never known a leader like that...

More wardens is what we need!!

We need more regulation, don't you see
And not bother planting another tree
More rules will keep us in line
And work and fear will fill up our time

Wardens to control our gas guzzling cars
And smoke wardens to patrol all our bars
Dog and park wardens are good too
They keep us in check for litter and poo

Keep all our children behind locked doors
And don't bother looking after our shores
But extend our shopping and drinking times
And make lots of money from gambling fines

We'll get wardens to control the bets and drinks
And make more money what do you think?
All the wardens will work very hard
And be issued with a special ID card

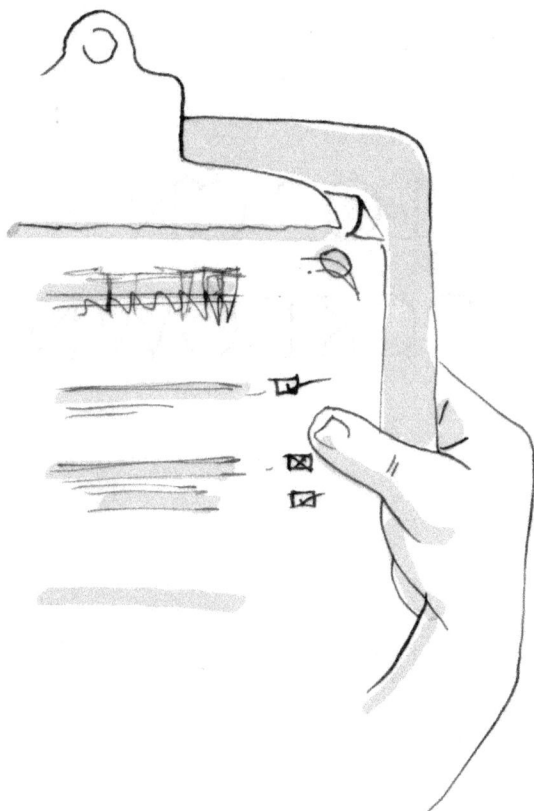

LOP ON
LOCKDOWN

Not on track

They want to lock us down
Keep us safe and never frown
Send our children back to schools
Like we are everybody's fools

We are 'ramping up' every day
We are testing in every way
No strategy or even a plan
They have no idea, not a single man

Families apart, people dying
Still we keep on trying
We will never get this time back
We are absolutely not on track

Don't let me forget

Don't let me forget what life used to be
When we were wild and free
We could laugh and meet
Even hug and greet
We could go out and dine
And everything would be fine
Don't let me forget…

Buster is Missing

My mum asked where has he gone?
She looked sad and quite forlorn
I asked who is this Buster guy?
You know, she gave a big sigh

It's not that Donald the Trump bloke
I wondered Buster? Before I spoke
For goodness sake you must know
He runs the country although he's slow

Ahhh... you mean the Boris man?
Yes, the one without the tan
I never see him so where is he?
I know Buster is missing, I agree

Don't drink the bleach

He trumped that bleach was the cure
The people thought odd… are you sure?
Now it is true bleach is good for poo and drains
But to drink it, might take your brains

It definitely needs to be carefully used
And bleach should never be abused
The people thought he was a strange colour
Bright orange that made them shudder
Maybe it was the bleach that made him this way
The people worried about it every day

The people thought this must be falsehood and lie
Still he ranted it's worth a try
Bleach is the answer he screeched and screeched
Don't listen in case you get bleached!

Lipstick on my mask

Wearing a mask is not revealing
People don't know how you are feeling
So I put a lipstick smile on mine
So people know I'm feeling fine
People waved and spoke to me
It made me happy don't you see

Then one day I put my mask on upside down
My lipstick smile turned to a frown
People now just pass me by
No longer talk or even try
My upside-down mask will stay this way
Until the virus goes away

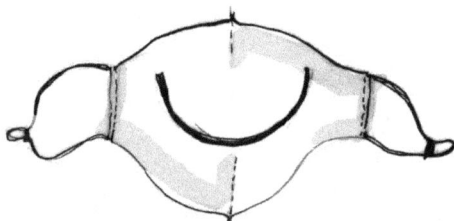

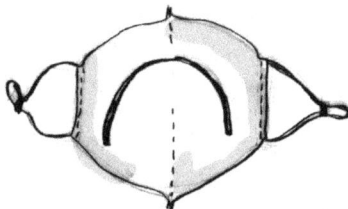

Wednesday is missing

My husband missed Wednesday
It seemed to have gone away
With every day looking the same way
Wednesday definitely went astray

He lost all week and complete track
I'm hoping a full week will come back
Then he mustered and returned
And Wednesday was once again found

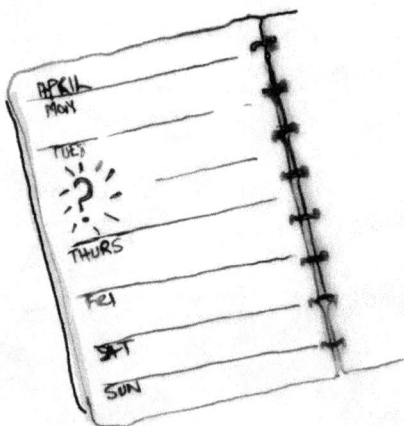

Busters' been found

My mum said he's been found
I thought he'd gone to ground
He's in Scotland don't you know
He should be working, the so-and-so

Still it's good that Buster has not gone away
He will come back soon so they say
He needs to get our children back to school
Not on holiday, what a fool

The dodgy knee (in lockdown)

The dodgy knee has a dodgy wrist
She gave it an almighty twist
I live many miles away
But my sister visits every day

Local heroes to be found
Kind people who don't go to ground
Still the knee is feeling better
All I could do was send a letter

We are in it together

This slogan doesn't seem right to me
I'm lucky with home, garden and an apple tree
But if I was left homeless
I would feel pretty hopeless
If I was a single mum, no garden and living high
I think my life would be one big sigh

I see people obediently wearing masks
I see politicians refusing this simple task
People stayed safe at home
While important folk went for a roam
This doesn't feel much together
Surely we can do so much better

I don't think

I don't think that people walk mile on mile
With sad children who never smile
I don't think people risk life and limb
Crossing seas for a passing whim

I know about the kinder train
Children rescued, not to blame
I don't think we've learned lessons past
I don't think we will last

The leg

We go walking every day
Hoping to keep the virus away.
The leg appeared on the first day
My friend and I thought no way

The dogs sniff and dig in the ground
And bring us what they have found
Four weeks the leg comes back
No matter whatever track

A ball was taken one day
But swapped for leg on the way
We said drop the leg on the spot
The dogs didn't give a jot

We threw it over wall
But that was no good at all
Next we kicked it in the burn
But still it made a return

We threw it over brambles and stiles
We threw it for miles and miles
Still from the very start, have a heart
The deer is missing an important part

Buster is back

Buster was missing, then found and now he's back
Made no difference still not on track
Weasel words that made no difference
They are all the same these politicians

My mum said it's not like the war
Nobody left through the back door
Buster must be trying his best you know
They duck and dive, they are so low

Still I'm glad he's not missing anymore
He's entertaining and not a bore
That's not the point, mum I said
We could easily all be dead

One planet

Our hands were washed and washed
Toilet rolls were neatly stashed
We cleaned everything in sight
It was a terrible plight

Never close and not a hug
We had to protect from the terrible bug
We couldn't hear, smell or even see it
We knew if we caught it, we wouldn't be fit

It tries to take our humanity away
But we will fight it in every way
This planet is for everyone
Russia, India and all under the sun

The lesson is clear we have one chance
We can all see at a glance
Human beings are all one race
Let's get together and embrace

Hope

It's a wonderful day
When things go your way
Apples are on the tree
And the rose is flowering free

A red squirrel skipped across the path
A robin splashed and took a bath
The chickens are laying eggs
The washing hangs on neat pegs

It's a wonderful day
When things go your way.

www.ingramcontent.com/pod-product-compliance
Lightning Source LLC
Chambersburg PA
CBHW031634040426
42452CB00007B/817